designwallas™